THE
SIGNIFICANCE
OF JESUS

BY

W. R. MALTBY, D.D.

Burwash Memorial Lectures, 1928

TORONTO
VICTORIA COLLEGE PRESS
STUDENT CHRISTIAN MOVEMENT PRESS
58 BLOOMSBURY STREET, LONDON, W.C.1

To

E. H. M.

First published, May, 1929
Second Edition, July, 1929
Third Edition, November, 1929
Fourth Edition, October, 1931

PRINTED IN GREAT BRITAIN BY
THE GARDEN CITY PRESS LTD., LETCHWORTH, HERTS

THE SIGNIFICANCE OF JESUS

WHS

INTRODUCTION

THE Committee in charge of the Burwash Memorial Lectureship congratulates itself on having secured as its third lecturer Rev. W. Russell Maltby, D.D.

Four of the addresses herein contained were given in the Chapel of Victoria University under the auspices of the Alumni of Emmanuel College, which is now the Theological College in Victoria University constituted of Union College (formerly Knox) and Victoria Faculty of Theology. It is needless to say these lectures awakened a profound interest. The Chapel was filled on all occasions. It would be difficult to over-estimate the religious values which Dr. Maltby brought to the Conference. In his visit to Canada Dr. Maltby did not confine himself to these lectures. He preached in the Convocation Hall of the University of Toronto, visited the societies of the Student Christian Association, and spoke at the prayer services of many of the Colleges. He also visited many University centres in Canada, and preached in many churches.

Henceforth many Canadians reading what Dr. Maltby writes, will do so with heightened interest as they recall the effective tones of his voice and the contagious influence of his religious faith.

R. P. BOWLES.

VICTORIA UNIVERSITY,
   IN THE UNIVERSITY OF TORONTO,
      October 5th, 1928.

NOTE

THE following Lectures were delivered in September last at the invitation of Chancellor Bowles and the Alumni of Emmanuel College, the Theological College of Victoria University, Toronto, to a very generous and indulgent audience, of whom I shall always retain grateful memories. Five Lectures were originally planned, of which the last would have been on "Jesus, the Saviour of Men." The occasion required only four Lectures and the Fifth was not written. This, however, was as it should be. If more was to be written on that high theme, it should be by a better hand than mine. I mention it here only lest anyone should think that I had joined the band of those who substitute the contemplation of a dead hero for the fellowship of a Living Lord. The road we travel in these Lectures does not end where they end. All the meanings we discover in the earthly life of Jesus deepen and converge to the mystery of His passion and shine out again in the glory of the Resurrection, but no doctrine of His Cross can dispense with the rich significance of His life.

W. R. M.

CONTENTS

CHAPTER I

JESUS YESTERDAY AND TO-DAY

THE seventy years of Biblical criticism through which we have passed must surely be reckoned among the major episodes in the history of the Christian Church. No other religion since the world began has undergone so fierce an intellectual ordeal, nor could any other have survived it. There are those who think that the whole trouble is due to the craft and subtlety of the devil, stirring up men in pride of knowledge to question the authority of the Church, or of the Bible, or both. But those who dissent from this strange notion and dare to think that even the *questioning* spirit is of God, must be willing to acknowledge that such times of unsettlement as we have lived through, have brought great distress to many minds, and chiefly to the non-combatants. For the protagonists on both sides had the exhilaration of combat and the occasional zest of victory, while the rank and file could do nothing but stand by and look on, doubtful at times if anything of the house of their faith would be left when the smoke of battle had cleared away. Half a dozen earthquakes or a considerable war would probably have involved less real suffering than the misery of doubt has occasioned to those whose heart and flesh cry out for the living God.

We may acknowledge all this, and still believe that something stronger than the hands of man or the subtlety of the devil is shaking the tabernacle of our faith. The mind of man, unless it is to be homeless and forlorn in a meaningless world, must build its own house, joining together the things it knows in some intelligible relation. The materials of its building are things known, things inferred, and things wished or feared, and we cannot be sure at every point what parts are permanent and what perishable. Nevertheless when we have built our house, we are in love with it, and we desire to rest from our labours and live in it. It is not only the believers who feel like this. Dr. Bertrand Russell having built his house, as he tells us, " on the firm foundation of unyielding despair," is just as resolute to defend it (though it seems a bleak site), as Mr. Gladstone was to defend his " impregnable rock of Holy Scripture." But God's wind and weather are always at work to search out the perishable elements in our structure, and time and again, when we longed only for finality and repose, we are required to rise and rebuild, or strengthen, or repair.

In the long controversy occasioned by modern Biblical criticism it is significant to notice how often the real issue has been mistaken on both sides. Orthodox apologists were often found fighting a rearguard action, evacuating by night what they defended by day. But it was not Christianity which they were defending at such times. In so far as they were contending for an infallible Book, the battle may be said to be definitely lost—and well lost, since an infallible book, whatever its conveniences, is an interdict on thinking, and therefore alien to the spirit of Christianity. Something better and richer than an infallible book is given to us both in the Old Testament and in the New.

In the Old Testament, as we now read it, we move in wider horizons than our fathers recognised. It is possible for us to watch there the patient ways of God with a strangely gifted race. We learn that revelation is not less truly God-given because it is not dictated but discovered. We can follow the conflict of true and false thoughts of God as they strove together in the minds of good men, and are now relieved of the hard necessity of thinking that God said all they thought He said. It is a great gain that we can see the prophets as men, and allow them to have second thoughts, and to correct and deepen their imperfect conceptions of God as experience taught them. Recovering the historical context of old prophetic words, we find them recharged with meaning, and in the wide sweep of moral law discover them to be relevant at once to their own time and to ours. But this newer way of reading the Old Testament presupposes something in the way of expert introduction—and some introducers, it must be admitted, do too much magnify their office—it requires some mental effort, some patience and a good deal of humility. And since many refuse to make this necessary contribution, they are apt to be left with a Bible vaguely suspect, and in the last push, uncertain everywhere.

The results of New Testament criticism have perhaps been less sensational, but they touch religion nearer to the heart. In the main they amount to a remarkable vindication of the genuineness and integrity of the documents.

Those of us who can remember the days when we clung firmly to the " four undisputed epistles " of St. Paul, and had to be content with arguments a little precarious for the dating of the synoptic Gospels *somewhere* in the first century, may well be thankful for the position as we find it to-day, when all the more important letters of St. Paul are sufficiently autographed, and the synoptic Gospels dated somewhere between the sixties and the eighties of the first century, with other documents of the like tenor reaching much further back.

The process by which the story of that unique life has been preserved to us is indeed utterly unlike anything which we should have expected, and if we still imagine that the more a process is human, the less it is divine, we shall find ourselves bewildered. We can watch those evangelists at work, collecting their materials, borrowing, eliminating, amplifying, in a free human way, with no paralysing thought that they were adding to the scriptures, or writing for all time. They have their limitations and their points of view. They give us fragments, and only fragments ; they are uncertain in their chronology and differ in the sequence of events ; they leave strange gaps and are careless about many things which we should give all our treasure to know.

But one thing they did not do. Neither by their art nor by their artlessness did they hide Jesus. From the deliberate contemplation of their records, there has been given to us in our day a fresh disclosure of Jesus. The experts still have their synoptic problem and it may occupy them for some time to come; and there are other questions of great moment on which scholars are not yet agreed. Nevertheless those who will, may see Jesus as no generation has seen Him since apostolic days.

There are many tokens that Jesus is again drawing the wondering eyes of men. One is to be found in the extraordinary output of books about Him—of which the more part are mercifully fallen asleep. Another token is to be found in the fact that the average man has begun to distinguish between Christ and Christianity, and to praise Christ at the expense of the religion which bears His name. All men speak well of Him now. This is good, though eager advocates should not make too much of it. It is a cheap thing to build the tombs of dead prophets. Once let it be understood that He whom we call Lord is safely buried nineteen centuries away, and there will be no lack of monuments. But in so far as this discrimination between Christ and His Church means that the significance of Jesus is challenging the attention of men in a new way, there is everything to be thankful for. And this is certainly true, both in Christian and in non-Christian countries. Someone describing the changing attitude of Indians toward the Christian message and Christian missionaries, traced three stages. First they said, Christianity is not *true*; then they said, Christianity is not *new*; now they say, Christianity is not *you*. Something like the same progress may be observed nearer home. Fragments of the teaching of Jesus are penetrating into unlikely quarters. Vexed with intractable social problems which will not solve *our* way, some have discovered that His way has never been tried, and some of His neglected sayings are found to be surprisingly relevant to our condition. Outside the bounds of the Christian Church, many are found ready to admit that He is the Light of the world, if there *is* a light of the world, and that He has the clue to the meaning of life, if there is a meaning. Starving for want of a little goodwill and peace with it, the modern world is more disposed to listen to

Him who spoke of it, possessed it and promised it to men. All this is to the good, and it may be the prelude to a movement toward God, deeper and stronger than anything as yet discernible among us. For if the Incarnation be the greatest thing done on earth, it must be a matter of infinite moment that that Incarnate Life should be presented to us as never before in its wholeness and simplicity, fresh, luminous, and inexhaustibly significant as we are finding it to be.

If we claim here that some significance of Jesus has been recovered for our day, that presumes that something had been lost, and it seems necessary to inquire how it came to be lost. To put our gains in a word, we have recovered the truth of the real humanity of our Lord. It is difficult to realise how largely this truth had been lost, even while it stood in the recited creeds, and called to men from the pages of the book they revered. Even now it is only beginning to enrich the experience and transform the outlook and conduct of Christian men. It came as a disturbing portent not a century ago, and the Church, not unnaturally, took up arms against it. For new truth never comes by way of mere addition to our stock, as though a new field were added to our farm.

Always the new truth shifts some old boundaries and this is why we usually go out to meet an unfamiliar truth with a gun in our hand. So this return of the Son of Man, if one may dare to call it so, came to disturb our imperfect theologies. The Church, of course, in its formal creeds has always asserted the true humanity as well as the deity of our Lord. But being more concerned to defend His divinity, which was always under the threat of attack, it fell into the way of affirming His divinity at the expense of His humanity, as though whatever was added to the one must be subtracted from the other. Accordingly those who showed unusual interest in the Man Christ Jesus came under suspicion of denying His divinity, and quite frequently the suspicion was justified. For this is the penalty which we must expect to pay for hesitating and intermittent loyalty to the truth, that others will neglect what we affirm in order to explore what we neglect. The Incarnation is indeed in the true sense a great mystery, and perhaps no one has really believed who has not first found it incredible. It has always been easier to surrender half the truth and to see Him either as a Man, even as the ideal Man, or else as a God who once for a little while wore the disguise of a human body.

B

The Church left the first alternative to the heretics, but fell into the second herself.

It is not too much to say that for centuries the Church was hardly in possession of the reality of our Lord's humanity, and therefore the synoptic Gospels lost the better part of their meaning. The Apostles' Creed taught men to say, *I believe in Jesus Christ His only Son our Lord, who was conceived by the Holy Ghost, born of the Virgin Mary, suffered under Pontius Pilate, Was crucified, dead and buried, He descended into Hell; The third day he rose again from the dead . . . "* passing straight, you observe, from the miraculous birth to the sacrificial death and victorious resurrection, without a word to record the significance of those thirty years, and especially those *three*. No doubt the Church had seized with a true instinct on the supreme moments of His revelation, but no modern student could be content to leave without a word of wonder and gratitude, those three crowded years of service, in which not one word or deed or gesture of Jesus fails to give us something that we could not afford to lose. Yet centuries of Christian literature followed the road indicated by the creeds, reproduced the same emphasis, and exhibited the same unconscious suppression.

The same scholars who grapple with the mighty arguments of St. Paul, and rise with him to the height of his theme, fall to the level of the commonplace when they come to the deeds of Christ, and are obliged to " spiritualise " them, to discover some " spiritual " analogy, before they can find interest in them or turn them to edification. By theological prepossessions of which they were only partly conscious, the Man Christ Jesus was hidden from them. Jesus was a divine mind in a human body. They were afraid to take seriously such words as those of St. Paul, that " though He was one in nature with God, He emptied Himself," or to follow the boldness of the writer to the Hebrews who returns again and again to the real humanity of our Lord, insisting that " it behoved Him to be made like His brethren in all respects," that " He Himself had experience of being tempted—tempted in all respects like ourselves, except for sin." Or still more daringly, " Having offered prayers and supplications with strong crying and tears and been heard because of His human piety, though He was a Son, yet He learned the lesson of obedience from His human experiences." Luther, indeed, broke out splendidly, " When I thus imagine Christ, then do I picture Him truly and properly. I grasp and have the true Christ, as He pictures Himself, and then I let go utterly all thoughts and speculations concerning the Divine Majesty and Glory, and hang and cling to the humanity of Christ ; then there is no fear there, but only friendliness and joy, and I learn thus through Him to know the Father."

But this was a voice crying in the wilderness. Christian interpreters thought of Jesus in the days of His flesh as equipped with all the resources of omniscience, and rejected the idea of any human limitations as though this were something dishonouring to Him. By so doing they removed from that Life almost all that makes human life what it is. They left no room for mental strife, for uncertainty, for ventures of faith, or indeed for faith at all, for surprise or disappointment, for suspense and frustration of plans. Temptation had no reality for Him, in any sense which we can understand. They did not *quite* do all this because the story was too strong and human for them, but the logic of their position pointed that way, and often they came near to bleaching all the colour and the wonder out of the one Perfect Life.

The story of the Temptation in the Wilderness is a crucial instance. A modern student finds in the account of the Temptation a clue to the whole ministry of Jesus and one of the most moving pieces of autobiography that literature affords. But none of the older commentaries has anything to say that is worth consulting on that episode. They did not apprehend its meaning and it simply did not interest them. They make such comment as they can, for it is the business of a commentator to comment, and apparently it is against the rules for him to say simply, " I do not understand this." We are told that the devil appeared "probably in a human form": that our Lord " dispersed the assaults of the adversary like smoke." " We have here," says Matthew Henry, " the story of a famous duel, fought hand to hand between Michael and the dragon, . . . and our Lord comes off a Conqueror, and so secures not only comfort but conquest at last to all his faithful followers." For such expositors, the Temptation falls to the level of a sham fight between an omniscient God and a not very subtle devil, and as this view leaves little to expound, they hasten on to edification. They draw improving lessons from the passage, as for instance, the desirability of being able to answer the temptations

of Satan in the words of scripture ; the wicked-
ness of the devil in not finishing his quota-
tions ; the virtue of fasting, in that our Lord
" dieted for the combat, as wrestlers who are
temperate in all things, but Christ beyond any
other, for He fasted forty days and forty
nights," a lesson which does not prevent the
same expositor from pointing out that the
fasting and consequent hunger left our Lord
peculiarly exposed to temptation. How ob-
vious it is that none of these useful lessons are
derived from the story of the Temptation but
are brought to it! It is pathetic that men intel-
lectually so greatly endowed and spiritually
of such insight and sympathy should have
visited that desert scene blindfold and left
nothing behind but a litter of tracts.

Dr. Sanday said that there was nothing
more authentic in the Gospels than the account of the Temptation. Turn and look at it
again. If we allow the Gospels to speak for
themselves we must regard the Baptism of
Jesus as an event which meant everything to
Him. We do not know what went before, in
those days when He must have known Himself different from other men—what strange
surmisings, momentary intimations, sudden
glimpses, what questions, and answers follow-

ing. But in that hour of the Baptism, after whatever preliminary preparation, He knew Himself the Beloved Son of the Father and the Anointed of God. The same voice which announced His unique relation to God gave Him to the service and redemption of men. The tension of spirit which inevitably followed from such an experience is surely reflected in those later words which He addressed to His disciples when He asked them if they were able to be baptised with the baptism which He Himself had experienced. It drove Him into solitude and the desert, there to think out His supreme and awful task, to ponder what was to be done, or, where that was hidden, what was not to be done.

The account of what happened there must have come from Himself, and in telling it He showed to His friends the inmost secret of His heart. As a treasure is put in a casket that it may be preserved, so the story of those weeks of mental strife is cast in a kind of symbolism, that it might be remembered through days when it could not be understood, for the benefit of the days when it could. The truth is half-hidden that we may search for it the more, but when we have searched, surely it is plain that here is the record of long days of sifting thought, of patient disentangling of confused issues, of resolute discrimination between the best and the good which is the enemy of the best—all in a region unvisited by man, undreamed of by any of His contemporaries. As told to us, there were three temptations coming in orderly succession, but it was Jesus who reduced those weeks of strenuous thought to this simplicity. Temptations of the deeper kind do not " in the onset come " thus arranged and simplified, and it needed all the patience and utter sincerity of Jesus Himself to control that chaos of possible courses, all speaking at once, to force each to declare itself and be known for what it was.

He was conscious of supernormal power entrusted to Him and the significant thing is that it brought to Him first the apprehension of its dangers and a rigorous scrutiny of the right and wrong ways of using it ; and for Jesus this meant a scrutiny of God's way of using power, for the Son could do nothing but what He saw the Father doing.

He might have turned stones into bread— for Himself in His hunger, and therefore afterwards for others too. He knew what hunger was, and does anyone suppose that that compassionate heart was easily reconciled to the hunger of men and women. He refused, seeing what it meant. Later, upon a great occasion He made the venture. According to all four Gospels, He fed the multitudes miraculously. A right response was within their power, but they did not so respond, and a few days later He was obliged to tell them that they were dishonoured, for they followed Him for what they could get. Whether we accept the miracle or explain it away, the lesson remains, for we can see it in the situation. He gave men healing and He could surely have given them nothing so unexceptionable. But in a very little while, His message and His mission were in danger of being drowned in the only kind of miracle they cared about. Frantic crowds were fighting to get near Him in order to be healed. They would drive Him to the dilemma either to heal no one or to do nothing but heal. They left Him nothing but a mere knife edge to walk upon, but He found the way, and the principle underlying all His action is the principle of that choice in the wilderness, men were to be won, not *bought*, not even with bread, not even with health.

In the second temptation,[1] He was offered the kingdoms of the world on condition of some

[1] I follow St. Luke's order. Luke iv, 5.

act of homage to the power that ruled them. The temptation was much more subtle and difficult than some interpretations would lead us to suppose, for there is a place even for force in God's scheme of things. It was within His power " to break oppression " and " rule in equity," and He knew that the story of oppression is more pitiful than even the records of hunger. But He would not fight the world with its own weapons. He refused the kingdom of the second-best, the kingdom of this world, because men were to be won, not coerced even by a beneficent omnipotence. Again, in the third temptation, He refused to overawe men, to give them the sign from Heaven, the overwhelming proof for which they asked. He would not remove the option of faith, though He knew how doubt can harry us and mystery pierce.

It is said that the devil departed from Him for a season, for His choice was made and it was final, but how often and in what subtle forms were the same temptations pressed upon Him by friends and foes alike. The temptations were not those which come to a base or an ambitious or a presumptuous nature. They found Him on the side where He was most vulnerable—on the side of His compassion.

Food so hard to find, justice so hard to come by, God so hard to know—it was the woes of the world which called to that mighty heart and He found it hard to withhold. He left hunger and oppression and doubt in the world, though He armed all His followers against them. They were not to be abolished by the mere fiat of power. Every stage in this progressive refusal of the second-best was an act of reverence toward the human personality, a determination to leave the bounds of moral freedom where God had placed them, and a deep consent to the patient ways of God, startling to us who are impatient of God's patience and resentful of the inexorableness of His love.

But with this clue in our hands, is it too much to say that the whole course of the Gospel records acquires a new unity and a most moving significance? The miracles of Jesus used to be regarded as one of the chief evidences of Christianity, but when the attack shifted, they became one of its difficulties. Even now, some apologists think their task would be simplified if this supernormal element could be eliminated. No solution will be found, I think, in that direction. The tide already is ebbing in that creek and no boat will float long in those waters. But however that may be, it is certainly a mistake to imagine that the question is one about miracles in general. It is *these* miracles with which we are concerned, and if we intend to deal with the data provided, we shall have to answer two questions, Why Jesus worked any miracles, and Why He did not work more. For on the records the second is as much a problem as the first. Jesus, we may say, worked miracles because men must see that God is Master in His own world, that our limitations are not His bounds, nor even ultimately *our* bounds.

But the practice of Jesus also shows us that when miracles no longer opened the heavens, but only closed men the more effectually in the prison of sense, when they could not be made sacramental, then He avoided the occasions of them. If they were not received as an outward and visible sign of a spiritual Presence and an infinite kindness, they were not blessings, but bribes. They did not show God; they hid Him. When the darkness fell on that first Sabbath in Capernaum, Jesus, we are told, was going from one to another of the sick folk and healing them. It must have seemed to those who were there that the kingdom of Heaven had already come. By the morning

fresh patients were ready for Him. But who
among the disciples was capable of inventing
what follows ? He was missing in the morning,
and when His friends found Him, to bring
Him back, He surprised them by turning His
back upon His opportunities. He gave the
word to go on to another place " that we may
preach the Gospel there also." No one but
Himself understood that He was maintaining
the proportion of His life work, setting His
mighty works in the context of His whole
message, and rescuing His mission from the
crowds which neither understood it nor cared
for it. When a village showed hostility His
most intimate disciples thought a little fire
from heaven would be a very salutary lesson.
They did not know what spirit they were of,
still less did they know their Master's spirit,
and it must often have seemed to them as if
He kept all the hardships for His friends and
spared only His enemies. Are there any words
of Jesus more moving, more haunting, more
profound than those words to Peter—Peter
with the sword in his hand, bloody and ineffec-
tual—" Do you not know that if it were to be
done that way, I could now ask my heavenly
Father and He would send me twelve legions
of angels." Whatever may be meant by

twelve legions of angels the purport is clear, that at a word He could free Himself if He would—and they were binding His wrists at that moment. Peter, and others broken-hearted like him, could only groan and ask within themselves why He did not call for the angels rather than permit this horrible thing to go on. If we can answer that question aright, we have a light to lighten the whole riddle of human history.

Right to the very end, and never more strikingly than in the difficult accounts of the Resurrection appearances, this unique bestowing and refraining confronts us. These gifts that cease when they would have become bribes, this power that stops short of coercion, these signs that persuade but never overwhelm, are the signature of Jesus on all His recorded deeds. The underlying principle is clear and intelligible now, though utterly uncomprehended then. He respected as no other has done the sanctity of the human personality, and He died rather than invade it, as He died in order to win it for God. " Behold I stand at the door and knock "—that is His word. It is not there that others are content to stand. Kings and captains have battered the door down. Priests have claimed right of

CHAPTER II

JESUS VALIDATING FAITH

FATHER MARTINDALE in *The Faith of the Roman Church* tells us with sufficient plainness what is the ground on which a Catholic's confidence is built. " The sentiments (of a Catholic) may account for his fervour in practising his Faith ; they may assist him to hold it with a new conviction : but they are not at all his reasons for believing that the Church's dogmas are true, or her commands right. A Catholic considers that he has cogent reasons for holding that the Roman Church is guaranteed by God to teach him only what is true, and to command him only what is right. He has then but to discover what she teaches and commands, and will proceed to believe the dogma, and obey the command, not only when he has no feelings about the matter, but when his feelings may be in a perfect tumult of opposition. . . . He does not believe a dogma because he sees very clearly what it means, nor because he thinks it would be useful, were it true. . . . He will, in short, think his personal feelings quite unimportant, since he may have good ones, or wrong ones, or none."

Words like these seem to most of us to belong to an alien world, and indeed the writer warns us that we shall find it so. Remembering some things which the Roman Church has at times " taught " and " commanded " one wonders by what mental process a distinguished scholar can repeat the claim that the Roman Church is " guaranteed by God to teach only what is true and to command only what is right." Cogent reasons would indeed be needed for a proposition which is to sustain the whole weight of the Christian Faith by guaranteeing the infallibility of any Church which history has known, and thereby making all other reasons superfluous or perilous. When we search for these " cogent " reasons, do we find anything but another instance how weak reasons become strong if we want them enough? Honest minds would never have maintained such a position except under some strong compulsion, and the compulsion has been, in part at any rate, the human hunger for certainty about God. Protestant Christians are apt to undervalue the immense advantage of a wide general consent to the truths of religion, because they are aware of its dangers. Like other good things, it has its danger, and because it is dangerous and threatens the vitality of religion, God sees to it that this consent is from time to time challenged and broken. But the times of this broken consent are difficult,—not so much for scholars who have the zest of theological reconstruction and the relish of discovering one another's infirmities, but for ordinary people, who, if they want religion at all, want it to live by, and not merely to think about. They look for reinforcement where they are suffering defeat, for the support of the divine Companionship, and the sense of some great end, which, even when dimly apprehended, redeems their lives from triviality and the curse of littleness. The desire for such enlargement of life finds its natural expression and its deepest confirmation in prayer, which may be the most significant thing that a man ever does. Now the critical mood from which our age cannot escape may easily disable us for devotion. If one conducts an argument for God, ever so successfully, the argument is not a good immediate preparation for prayer. We live in an atmosphere of question and debate, and the questions often survive the answers, even when the answers have been good, and return to haunt the mind with vague uncertainties. There have been times in the past when those who sought God could find His temple not far away, and entering there, hear no discordant cries nor the echoes of debate, but only the testimony of many voices, made soft by distance, made sweet perhaps by death, all certifying that God was there. There one might leave off striving and surrender oneself to the encompassing Presence. If we were more childlike we might still find it true oftener than we do. But it is undeniable that for many it is not so. God seems hard to find. The questions of the mind being once raised cannot merely be put aside. Those who have once tasted intellectual freedom and know it to be the gift of God cannot take God on authority or assume Him for convenience sake. They cannot make the Christian affirmations, tremendous as they are, in the face of doubts which are not the doubts of pride or perversity, until they have found their way to some reasonable answer. It is no help to such perplexed minds to plead the authority of the Church or of the Bible, for the questions that rack the mind go back further and reach down deeper than the nature of the Church or the inspiration of the Bible. The doubt is rather as to the reality of a spiritual world and a personal God.

Of course, it is true that our fundamental difficulty with religion is to be honest enough to entertain it. This difficulty cannot be vicariously handled. Every man must deal with it himself. Many attempts have been made to construct a religion guaranteed to pass intact from father to son. But none of these attempts to gather a flock of unlosable sheep succeeds in the end. If we are to be religious we must have the chance of being irreligious. This is the will of God and not all the clergy and ministers of all denominations can make it otherwise, if they would. But this fundamental personal difficulty, insepar- able from moral freedom, is complicated and aggravated if religion is presented to us con- fused by any self-contradiction or in any way inadequate to known facts. Once more the task is presented to this generation of showing the Christian faith in its essential beauty, wholeness and simplicity, and therefore with an inherent authority of its own. There is, I believe, already within reach a nobler, more reasonable, more comprehensive message than even our fathers knew,—and this not because we are wiser, or even more sincere than they, but because it is not for nothing that the Spirit of God has been at work upon the minds of men during these years of amazing research and fearless interrogation. That better message, however, has not been so articulated as to reach the average man, and if he asks only where or how to begin, he may have to wait long before he hears any satisfying answer.

If we reject the Catholic reply and refuse to answer uncertainty by authority we ought not to make the mistake of treating the craving for certainty as if it were something illicit or merely the weakness of uninstructed minds. Some of the learned do not seem to understand this hunger of the human spirit. They think it sufficient to base religion on a balance of probabilities and are satisfied if they emerge from the argument for God with the honours on His side,—or theirs. They do not see why we should not be content to live, for a few years at any rate, with God as a tenable hypothesis. Perhaps religion is for some men mainly a subject of investigation and its questions an exhilarating employment for the mind. But religion was not given to enable the wise and prudent to complete their intellectual scheme, and no religion is more intolerant than Christianity of provisional acceptance. Those whose heart and flesh cry out for the living God can no more be content with uncertainty about Him than they could be content to be uncertain whether their dearest friend was dead or alive. The contention of these pages is that if we look at Jesus some certainties stand clear. He is the Way.

It may be convenient first to summarise the argument which I am to submit.

1. Spiritual realities, if there are such things, as religion affirms, must be spiritually discerned. Whatever else this involves it means that there are moral conditions for spiritual vision.

2. The conditions of spiritual vision are not fulfilled in us, and it is not therefore surprising or mysterious that we discern these spiritual realities dimly and doubtfully.

3. But the conditions were fulfilled in Jesus, and His testimony, if it is accessible to us, is valid evidence of the reality of the spiritual world, and a real starting point for a personal faith, a real beginning of personal communion with God.

1. There are moral conditions for spiritual vision. This is not a dogma to be accepted on authority. If it is not self-evident, it needs only a little honest attention for anyone to see it to be true. We know, for instance, that in the appreciation of beauty something more spiritual, shall we say, is required than mere keenness of sight. A hawk may see a landscape better than I, but it cannot see what I see. I can see a sunset, but I cannot see what Turner saw,—although Turner can teach me to see better. It is obviously the same with moral excellence of any kind. Some men simply do not know what honour means. Self-centred people are not usually conscious of their selfishness, and when they attain to any degree of proficiency in their self-regarding habit, do not know love when they see it. The classical instance is the elder son in the parable, who full of his own behaviour looks round upon a home and sees nothing but rivals who come off better than himself. Even with an elementary virtue like honesty the same rule holds. The men who appropriate other people's money and are found out, almost always think themselves ill-used and blame everyone except themselves. " The blindness which is induced by all deliberate